W9-CXU-187

I Dig Dinosaurs

WELDON OWEN PTY LTD

Publisher: Sheena Coupe
Senior Designer: Kylie Mulquin
Editorial Coordinators: Sarah Anderson,
Tracey Gibson
Production Manager: Helen Creeke
Production Assistant: Kylie Lawson

Project Editor: Ariana Klepac
Designer: Patricia Ansell
Text: Jan Stradling

05 04 03 02
10 9 8 7 6 5 4 3 2

© 2000 Weldon Owen Inc.
All rights reserved. No part of this publication
may be reproduced or transmitted in any form
or by any means, electronic or mechanical, including
photocopying, recording, taping, or any information
storage and retrieval system, without permission
in writing from the publisher.

Published in the United States by
Wright Group/McGraw-Hill
19201 120th Avenue NE, Suite 100
Bothell, WA 98011
www.WrightGroup.com

Printed in Singapore
ISBN: 0-7699-1220-6

CREDITS AND ACKNOWLEDGMENTS

PICTURE AND ILLUSTRATION CREDITS
[t=top, b=bottom, l=left, r=right, c=center]
Ad-Libitum/M.Kaniewski 15b. **Simone End** 19t. **Christer Eriksson** 3r, 5c. **John Francis/Bernard Thornton Artists UK** 7c. **Murray Frederick** 17tc, 17tl. **Lee Gibbons/Wildlife Art Ltd** 20–21. **David Kirshner** 11c, 18t. **Frank Knight** 17l. **David McAllister** 19b. **James McKinnon** 4tl, 6t, 16c. **Photodisc** banding. **Luis Rey/Wildlife Art Agency** 1c, 4bl, 8–9c, 9cr. **Peter Schouten** 5tr, 8bl, 9tr, 9br, 10t, 12b, 13–14, 22.

Weldon Owen would like to thank the following people for their assistance in the production of this book:
Peta Gorman, Michael Hann, Marney Richardson.

Contents

What Is a Dinosaur?   4

Dinosaur Times   6

Meat Eaters   8

Plant Eaters   10

Parade of Dinosaurs   12

What Is a Fossil?   14

Dinosaur Fossils   16

Where Did They Go?   18

Glossary   20

What Is a Dinosaur?

Dinosaurs were *reptiles.* They laid eggs. Their skin was scaly and waterproof. They walked with their legs tucked under their bodies.

Did You Know?

The word "dinosaur" means "terrible lizard."

The Komodo dragon
is the world's largest
living lizard. Unlike
a dinosaur,
its legs grow
on the sides
of its body.

Tyrannosaurus rex

5

Dinosaur Times

Dinosaurs lived millions of years ago. There were many different kinds. Some were bigger than a bus. Others were no bigger than a chicken.

Meat Eaters

Some dinosaurs only ate meat. They had sharp claws and teeth. They were strong and fast. They often ate other dinosaurs.

Dilophosaurus had sharp teeth.

Dinner Tools

Compsognathus used its hands to catch and eat lizards.

Gallimimus had a sharp, narrow beak for snapping up small animals and insects.

Baryonyx had very sharp claws. It used them just like fishhooks.

Tyrannosaurus rex was one of the biggest meat eaters.

Stegosaurus ate ferns and other plants.

Plant Eaters

Some of these plant eaters had long necks to reach the tops of trees. They walked through forests looking for food.

Parade of Dinosaurs

Some dinosaurs were big
and slow and some
were small
and fast. Some
walked on two legs.
Some walked on four legs.

Triceratops

Camptosaurus

Allosaurus

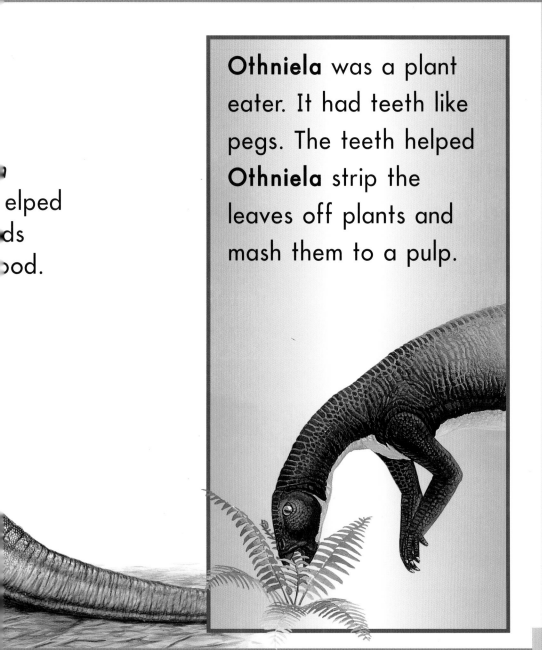

Othniela was a plant eater. It had teeth like pegs. The teeth helped **Othniela** strip the leaves off plants and mash them to a pulp.

elped
ds
ood.

Stomac
stones
sauropo
digest f

stomach stones

Saltasaurus

Corythosaurus

Tyrannosaurus

Pachycephalosaurus

Euoplocephalus

Stegosaurus

Coelurus

Some dinosaurs had
spikes, horns,
and bony plates.
These *protected* them
against enemies.

Make a Dinosaur Mobile

1. Choose your three favorite dinosaurs on this page.
2. Draw them on a piece of cardboard.
3. Color them on both sides and cut them out.
4. Punch a hole in the top center of each dinosaur.
5. Put three different lengths of string through the holes and tie them to a stick.
6. Hang up your mobile.

What Is a Fossil?

When some dinosaurs died, sand and mud started to cover their bodies. After a very long time, the bones turned into rock. This rock is called a *fossil*.

Sometimes footprints became fossils.

How a Fossil Is Made

A dinosaur dies.

Sand and mud cover skeleton and harden into rock.

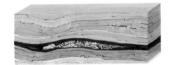

Bones slowly turn to rock.

The fossil is uncovered.

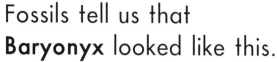

Fossils tell us that
Baryonyx looked like this.

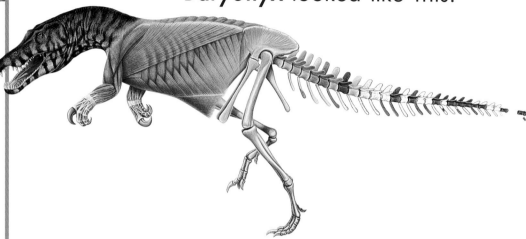

Dinosaur Fossils

Fossils tell us about the shape
and size of dinosaurs. Sometimes
fossils of other animals are found
in a dinosaur's stomach. This tells
us what the dinosaur ate.

Did You Know?

We will never know for sure what color dinosaurs were.

Digging for fossils is hard work.

Where Did They Go?

Nobody knows what happened to dinosaurs. Some people think a *meteorite* hit the Earth. Others think the weather changed or a volcanic eruption kept sunlight from reaching the Earth.

Glossary

fossil The remains of an animal or plant from long ago, preserved as rock.

meteorite A lump of stone or metal that has fallen to Earth from space.

protect To guard or defend.

reptile An animal covered in scales who breathes air through lungs, and whose body heat changes as the temperature around it changes.

stomach stones Stones in some animals' stomachs that help grind up food.